TIME

A practical guide to

WELL

developing your daily devotions

SPENT

COLIN WEBSTER

TIME

A practical guide to

WELL

developing your daily devotions

SPENT

COLIN WEBSTER

10 Publishing
a division of 10ofthose.com

Copyright © 2021 by Colin Webster

First published in Great Britain in 2021

The right of Colin Webster to be identified as the Author of this Work has been asserted by him in accordance with the Copyright, Designs and Patents Act 1988.

British Library Cataloguing in Publication Data
A record for this book is available from the British Library

ISBN: 978-1-913896-07-2

Designed and typeset by Pete Barnsley (CreativeHoot.com)

Printed in the UK

10Publishing, a division of 10ofthose.com
Unit C, Tomlinson Road, Leyland, PR25 2DY, England

Email: info@10ofthose.com
Website: www.10ofthose.com

1 3 5 7 10 8 6 4 2

Psalm 19:7–14

The law of the LORD is perfect,
    refreshing the soul.
The statutes of the LORD are trustworthy,
    making wise the simple.
The precepts of the LORD are right,
    giving joy to the heart.
The commands of the LORD are radiant,
    giving light to the eyes.
The fear of the LORD is pure,
    enduring for ever.
The decrees of the LORD are firm,
    and all of them are righteous.
They are more precious than gold,
    than much pure gold;
they are sweeter than honey,
    than honey from the honeycomb.
By them your servant is warned;
    in keeping them there is great reward.
But who can discern their own errors?
    Forgive my hidden faults.
Keep your servant also from wilful sins;
    may they not rule over me.

Then I will be blameless,
>	innocent of great transgression.

May these words of my mouth and this
meditation of my heart
>	be pleasing in your sight,
>>	Lord, my Rock and my Redeemer.

CONTENTS

INTRODUCTION

During my days at Moorlands Bible College in Bournemouth, I used to beg a lift from a fellow student who had a car. He picked up one other student called John, along the way. After first introducing myself to John, I was somewhat taken aback when, after only a few moments, he asked me, 'So, how are your Quiet Times then?' I don't know what you would have replied but I hesitantly said, 'OK, I suppose – as normal as anyone else's, I guess!' and quickly changed the subject of conversation. To be honest, I was actually rather embarrassed that he asked me that question – but why? I think the answer is that Quiet Times – devotional times – are often so personal and private that we rarely, if ever, discuss them with anyone else. John's question was like having an intruder enter my home uninvited and rummage through my personal belongings!

For instance, if you are married, do you know what your husband's or your wife's Quiet Time is like? What about your best friend in church? Do you ever speak about it? Probably not. It's with this in mind that I have written down some gleanings from my own Quiet Times to take the lid off this best-kept secret.

Whether you are a new Christian or a mature believer, I hope you will find this book fuels your desire to set aside time to be alone with God. God's greatest desire is that you develop your relationship with him in order to become mature in your faith. Establishing a regular devotional life will also help you flourish as a believer so that you stand *out* as well as *up* for the Lord in this world. May you enjoy every precious moment spent at the feet of your Creator as you search his Word so that you become more like Jesus and serve him with joy.

1

WHAT IS A QUIET TIME?

The first time I heard the term 'Quiet Time' was from a young Zimbabwean called Simon Miller-Kranko, who at that time was training to be a hotel manager in London. As he began telling me something the Lord had taught him during his Quiet Time, I remember stopping him and asking, 'What's one of those?' Up until that point I never knew what to call my daily time of Bible reading and prayer. (In much the same way I never knew what to call the dangly thing hanging down from the back of my throat until I married a doctor. Incidentally, it's called the uvula!)

Put simply, a Quiet Time is time deliberately set aside in our day for seeking God as we prayerfully engage with his Word.

To aid our concentration, we need to remove ourselves from everything that would distract us. That means switching off the TV, radio or mobile phone (you'll survive!), and withdrawing to a quiet place away from every other competing voice. The aim of our Quiet Time is to focus on what God wants to say to us from the Bible and allow him to speak into our lives. It's the most important appointment of our day.

It's fair to say that most Christians struggle with their Quiet Times, myself included, so I do not have the spiritual high ground in this area. Our Quiet Times are full of ups and downs because we inevitably experience seasons of life which can be particularly demanding on us both physically and mentally. Everything from work demands, family circumstances or ill health can impact upon our devotional life, and we need to bear that in mind.

This short book will not be a magic wand that automatically sets you up with a great devotional life. I used to purchase Christian books with snappy titles, thinking that they would be a 'quick fix' to intimacy with the Almighty, requiring little or no effort from me.

But I soon discovered that if my walk with God was going to change, then it was going to take time, effort and commitment on my part. We don't like those three words because we live in such an instant world with its instant coffee, instant communication and instant results. Yet there is no product on the market which provides you with intimacy with God 'on the cheap'. Jesus didn't allow his disciples any shortcuts to intimacy with him, so we can't expect it either. Our relationship with God will only flourish if we invest time, effort and commitment.

QUIET TIME QUESTIONS

Are you keeping a regular Quiet Time? If not, what is hindering you? Are those hindrances avoidable or unavoidable? Do you think that in your busy life there is a part of your day that could be set aside in order to spend quality moments with God?

2

FIVE GOOD REASONS FOR HAVING A QUIET TIME

There are five good reasons for setting aside time to be with God.

1. TO SEEK AND THIRST AFTER GOD

Many years ago, at the church where I was working, I led a session on Quiet Times for the youth group. The young people were asked to share something of their own devotional experiences with the rest of the group. One young man, who hadn't been a Christian for all that long, piped up, 'I have stopped trying to get through my Quiet Time and started to seek God during my Quiet Time!' It was so simple a statement and yet I knew in my own heart that I was guilty of this. Unconsciously I had made it my goal simply to get through a chapter of the Bible, rather than to meet God by letting him speak into my life from his Word.

Sometimes we are so focused on completing our Bible reading that we can miss encountering God. All we have achieved is to fulfil our own Bible reading vows for that day. Yet the purpose of a Quiet Time is to meet with God. If we miss that, then we have missed the whole point!

Jesus gave this invitation to the crowds that gathered round him during the Feast of Tabernacles: 'Let anyone who is thirsty come to me and drink. Whoever believes in me, as Scripture has said, rivers of living water will flow from within them' (John 7:37–38). What the original Greek language actually implies here is this: 'If anyone is thirsty, let him *keep coming* to me and *keep drinking*!' (italics mine). It is a continuous process, so we need to continually, daily seek an encounter with the living God. As A.W. Tozer once said; 'Contemporary Christians have been caught in the spurious logic that those who have found God, no longer need to seek Him.'[1] Yet the truth of the matter is that those who know him are those who continue to seek him.

> ## QUIET TIME QUESTIONS
>
> Has your Quiet Time turned into a task to get through or is it an encounter with the living God? Is there anything that you need to change in your current Quiet Time structure that might bring freshness to it?

2. IT IS AN INCREDIBLE PRIVILEGE

The Apostle Peter wrote, 'For Christ also suffered once for sins, the righteous for the unrighteous, to bring you to God' (1 Pet. 3:18). Jesus has made the impossible possible. He has provided the way for sinful, flawed people to enter into God's holy presence.

In ancient times the temple, which dominated the city of Jerusalem, was the focal point for worshipping God. Every morning and evening priests would sacrifice offerings to atone for the

---

[1.] Stephen Eyre, *Time with God* (IVP, 1995), p. 36.

people's sins. Only the priests could offer such sacrifices by entering the inner sanctuary known as the Holy Place. Yet within the Holy Place, hidden behind a vast curtain, there lay an even more sacred room called the Most Holy Place (or Holy of Holies). This was where the Ark of the Covenant rested and where God's presence on earth dwelt. The only person who could ever enter here was the High Priest, and even then on only one very special day each year called the Day of Atonement. On that day the sins of the whole nation of Israel would be atoned for by the sacrifice of an innocent lamb without spot or blemish (Ex. 30:10). The Israelites couldn't just amble into the presence of God, with their hands in their pockets, whistling. Far from it, they had a deep and reverent fear of God, and entering his presence was both costly and a privilege.

The Gospel accounts remind us of that cost. When Jesus died on the cross, the curtain in the temple was torn in two from top to bottom. Christ's death provided the way whereby God was allowing people access to enter into his holy presence. That's an incredible privilege! We must never lose sight of the cost which

Jesus paid to purchase that privilege for us (see Heb. 4:14–16; 10:19–22).

QUIET TIME QUESTIONS

Are you taking advantage of the privilege which Christ's death has purchased for you? Why not thank God now that he doesn't keep you at arm's length but yearns for you to draw near to him.

3. BECAUSE OF OUR SOCIETY

In his book *Time with God*, Stephen Eyre points out the effect our society has upon us as believers:

In every aspect of society we are slowly institutionalising the absence of God. As Christians we lament this. But while we lament it we are being damaged by it. Like everyone else, we go through each day with little occasion to call upon God. Unless we take conscious precautions, we too slip into a pattern of spiritual darkness. Despite our best intentions or even the depth of our convictions,

we are affected. Like oxygen on metal, slowly,
imperceptibly, the effect of our culture is to rust
our souls.[2]

Let's be honest: there is very little in the outside world or in our workplace that naturally causes us to dwell on God. After all, how many of your work colleagues hum 'Blessed Be Your Name' by Matt Redman as they sit at the office desk? How many have a calendar with Bible verses pinned to their wall? Probably none. Our society rarely affirms God, nor does it stimulate our minds to consider him. We therefore need to dwell on him in advance, prior to entering this godless, spiritual desert, or our souls will 'rust'.

Three thousand years ago King David wrote, 'You, God, are my God, earnestly I seek you; I thirst for you, my whole being longs for you, in a dry and parched land where there is no water' (Ps. 63:1). That's how we ought to view our world – as a dry and weary land where there is nothing that would naturally refresh our soul. And because we cannot change our environment, we need to equip ourselves in

---

[2] Stephen Eyre, *Time with God* (IVP, 1995), p. 20.

order to survive it. In much the same way that a camel has to carry its own water supply because its natural environment is desert, we have to fill our thoughts with God. We need to be drinking in draughts of spiritual refreshment prior to entering our society's godless desert. For God's Word alone breathes reviving life into our weary hearts and combats this 'rusting of our souls'.

QUIET TIME QUESTIONS

What things can you identify in our society that cause a rusting of your soul? Pray about these. How might you better equip yourself to thrive and not just survive in a godless society?

4. IT AFFECTS US

The Apostle Paul, writing to his young companion Timothy, had this to say about the Bible: 'All Scripture is God-breathed and is useful for teaching, rebuking, correcting and training in righteousness, so that the servant of God may be thoroughly equipped for every good work'

(2 Tim. 3:16–17). The Bible is meant not merely to inform us but to transform us. It enables us to grow in our understanding of God and to become more Christ-like, mature and useful in God's kingdom. That's God's purpose for his Word. The benefits of reading the Bible are expressed on the Gideons International website in this way: 'Read it to be wise, believe it to be safe, and practice it to be holy. It contains light to direct you, food to support you, and comfort to cheer you. It is the traveller's map, the pilgrim's staff, the pilot's compass, the soldier's sword and the Christian's charter.'

Our devotional life affects us. We may not feel so at the time, but God is doing an invisible work within us. For through the Word of God, the Holy Spirit is chiselling away at our hearts and shaping them to become more like Christ. If we are engaging with God's Word sincerely, he has promised that he will not allow his Word to return to him empty (Is. 55:11).

This is often my own experience. My morning Bible reading has regularly provided godly wisdom for a situation or circumstance which I faced later that day, helping me to make the right choice. At other times the Lord has challenged me about a wrong attitude towards a person. And as I have submitted to his Word, I have found myself responding in a more gracious way than I would otherwise have done. Someone once said, 'Scriptures that are never read will never help us.'

QUIET TIME QUESTIONS

Have you given up on Quiet Times because you didn't seem to get much from them, or because God didn't get much cooperation from you?

5. IT CAN BENEFIT OTHERS

A regular devotional life also has the benefit of giving you a word of encouragement or wisdom to pass on to someone else. On many occasions I have found an encouragement gleaned from my morning Quiet Time has provided me with a pertinent word of blessing to share with another person later that day. That word proved to be as much for them as it was for me.

Yet I had no idea that what I was soaking into my own heart in the morning would be wrung out to refresh another person's weary soul by the afternoon.

The Apostle Paul speaks of sharing with others what we ourselves have received from God in his second letter to the believers in Corinth. He writes, 'Praise be to the God and Father of our Lord Jesus Christ, the Father of compassion and the God of all comfort, who comforts us in all our troubles, so that we can comfort those in any trouble with the comfort we ourselves receive from God' (2 Cor. 1:3–4).

More often than not, this comfort will have stemmed from our own reading and meditation on God's Word. God may be wanting to speak into your life something from his Word that could benefit another believer. As you share in this way, you will find this proverb to come true: 'As iron sharpens iron, so one person sharpens another' (Prov. 27:17). Someone else once observed, 'Encouragement costs you nothing to give, but it is priceless to receive.'

QUIET TIME QUESTIONS

Have you ever thought that your Quiet Time today might provide an encouragement for someone else tomorrow?

3

JESUS' QUIET TIME

Have you ever wondered what Jesus' Quiet Times were like? I have. We catch a glimpse of Jesus' own devotional life in Mark's Gospel:

Very early in the morning, while it was still dark, Jesus got up, left the house and went off to a solitary place, where he prayed. Simon and his companions went to look for him, and when they found him, they exclaimed: 'Everyone is looking for you!'

Jesus replied, 'Let us go somewhere else – to the nearby villages – so that I can preach there also. That is why I have come.' So he travelled throughout Galilee, preaching in their synagogues and driving out demons (Mark 1:35–39).

We observe four things about Jesus' Quiet Time from this passage.

1. THE TIME (V. 35)

It was early in the morning! Now if you are a student, teenager or someone who struggles to rise in the morning, you won't like the first word in that passage – it actually says 'very early' in the morning! Yet it seems that this was Jesus' usual routine. The prophet Isaiah wrote concerning the Messiah: 'The Sovereign LORD has given me a well-instructed tongue, to know the word that sustains the weary. He wakens me morning by morning, wakens my ear to listen like one being instructed' (Is. 50:4). Luke speaks of another occasion when Jesus rose early: 'At daybreak, Jesus went out to a solitary place' (Luke 4:42). We are clearly given the impression that morning by morning Jesus spent time alone listening to his heavenly Father. He was seeking his blessing and instruction for the day that lay ahead (John 5:19; 6:38; 8:28). If Jesus made it a priority to spend time with his heavenly Father before launching out into his busy day, shouldn't we?

The great Scottish preacher Robert Murray McCheyne once wrote this advice to a young student training for the ministry: 'Above all, keep much in the presence of God. Never see the face of man till you have seen His face who is our life, our all.' That is the essence of a private devotion: to seek the face of God before we seek the face of anyone else.

2. HIS MENTAL CONDITION (V. 35)

He was awake! Jesus was fully dressed and had a sharp mind. He wasn't giving his heavenly Father the groggy fag ends of his time and energy. His mind was clear not cloudy. He was giving the freshest moments of his day to his Father.

One of the reasons people don't benefit properly from their Quiet Time is precisely because their minds are not capable of retaining anything – they are too tired! Have you ever found yourself at the end of a weary day slipping into bed, extending an arm to the bedside table, picking up your Bible and beginning your Quiet Time? How many of those devotions have ended up being eight hours long, interrupted only by the sound of the alarm clock going off as it wakes you up from a deep sleep? Give God the best of everything in your life, including the sharpness of your mind.

3. THE PLACE (V. 35)

He went to a solitary place with few distractions. Jesus did his utmost to withdraw from anything that would compete with undisturbed fellowship with his heavenly Father. For many of us, our greatest distraction will be our mobile phones, which we constantly check for updates of news and messages. I suggest that you switch your phone off completely or place it in another room to prevent unwanted interruptions.

I appreciate that for people who have young children, solitude can seem impossible, but others have found a way. Susanna Wesley for example, had a unique way of letting her young children know that she required undisturbed time with God. She would sit down in a comfy chair and pull an apron over her head, and in those brief moments she would pray to the Lord. Eventually her children learned that no matter how much they yelled, when their mum had that apron over her head, she was not to be disturbed!

4. THE REASON (VV. 38–39)

Jesus needed to be alone with his Father because he had a busy day ahead! Indeed, Jesus had been busy the night before too – read Mark 1:32–34. No one had a tighter schedule than Jesus. He had only three years in which to complete all the divine appointments that his Father had arranged for him. Yet despite the obvious demands and needs of those surrounding him, he deliberately withdrew from the crowds in order to be alone with this Father. If Jesus needed to spend time with his Father every day, despite his heavy schedule, so do we!

4

WHAT ELEMENTS MAKE UP A QUIET TIME?

There are three elements that go into my Quiet Time.

1. PREPARATION

We saw from Jesus' own devotional life that he withdrew to a solitary place to spend time with his heavenly Father, away from any distractions. My quiet, solitary place is a comfortable chair overlooking our garden (with a cup of coffee of course!). During the summer months I relocate outside into the garden itself. Wherever your quiet place happens to be, might I suggest again that you switch off your mobile phone from any distracting alerts which could rob you of quality time with God.

I always take a few moments prior to looking at my Bible to reflect on whose presence I am entering. This helps to prepare my heart to receive from God. I remind myself that God is right there with me, as King David reminded himself when he wrote, 'I keep my eyes always on the LORD. With him at my right hand, I shall not be shaken' (Ps. 16:8).

I personally find it helpful to begin with a short moment of stillness, followed by a brief prayer. I should point out that I rarely pray out loud during my devotions. I simply pray silently in my own heart to the Lord (as God hears our thoughts as clearly as any spoken word). I find I'm able to articulate far more to him this way than if I have to carefully construct verbalised sentences.

It's worth taking a few moments to orientate your heart and mind to the majesty and greatness of God. Remember whose presence you have the privilege to enter through the merits of Christ. Approach God in the certain knowledge that you are dearly loved by him and have been invited to draw near to him. Praise God for who he is and for what he has done in your life. Worship him for his attributes. Marvel at the wonder of his creation. Thank him for his provision to you in so many ways. Rejoice that your eternal salvation is secure in Christ.

You may find reading a few verses from a psalm helps you start this time of praise. Alternatively, you may like to read the words to a favourite hymn or listen to a worship song. There is a wealth of worship resources that can assist your heart and mind to focus on the Lord.

I sometimes read a short daily devotion from Charles Spurgeon's famous *Morning and Evening* prior to my Bible reading. In a way I regard Spurgeon's devotionals as a spiritual tow aeroplane. A tow plane pulls a glider (which has no engine of its own) up into the sky, then when it reaches a certain altitude, the tow plane releases the cable so that the glider can soar on its own and appreciate the view. Well first thing in the morning my cloudy mind can often feel like that powerless glider. But as I read Spurgeon's short pastoral passage, I find myself instantly pulled up to admire the spiritual scenery of our glorious God. On many an occasion Spurgeon's reflections have helped prime the pump of my devotions. His *Morning and Evening* devotions are available on various apps as well as in book form.

2. READING AND REFLECTING ON THE BIBLE

The Apostle Paul said, 'All Scripture is God-breathed and is useful for teaching, rebuking, correcting and training in righteousness, so that the servant of God may be thoroughly equipped for every good work' (2 Tim. 3:16–17).

The Bible is utterly unique. There is no other book that you can read where the author is present in the room with you! The Holy Spirit inspired the Scriptures, therefore he is the one who can illuminate our minds as we read God's Word. This is why I always begin my Bible reading by asking the Lord to help me understand his Word by the power of his Holy Spirit. Then, during my Bible reading, I find that the Holy Spirit highlights a verse or a word which brings to mind a fresh challenge or insight. As I meditate on a verse, I find that my heart is either comforted, encouraged, warned or instructed.

And as I take that instruction to heart and apply it in my life, I am enabled to grow in my maturity and relationship with the Lord.

George Müller was a great man of prayer who lived in the nineteenth century. He wrote this about his devotional life:

The first thing I did, after having asked in a few words the Lord's blessing upon His Word, was to begin to meditate on the Word, searching as it were into every verse to get blessing out of it; not for the sake of preaching on what I had meditated on, but for the sake of obtaining food for my own soul. The result I have found to be almost invariably this, that after a very few minutes my soul has been led to confession, thanksgiving, intercession, or supplication, so that though I did not, as it were, give myself to prayer, but to meditation, yet it turned almost immediately into prayer. When thus I have been for a while making confession, intercession or supplication, or having given thanks, I go on to the next words or verse, turning all as I go on into prayer for myself or others, as the word may lead to it, but still continually keeping before me that food for my own soul is the object of my meditation. The result of this is that there is always a good deal of confession, intercession etc. mixed with my meditation, and that my inner man is invariably nourished and strengthened, and that by breakfast time, with rare exceptions, I am in a peaceful and happy state of heart.[3]

If we, like Müller, keep a prayerful approach to the reading of Scripture, we too will find that Bible reading and praying will intertwine with each other quite naturally. Indeed, meditation on the Word will actually provide fuel for our prayers. For example, if I am reading Paul's prayer for the believers in Colossae (see Col. 1:9–14) and pray these qualities into my own life, I may then use that same passage to fuel my prayers for a new believer in my church. In this way I use Paul's prayer as a template to flesh out my own prayers for someone else.

[3.] George Müller, *A Narrative of Some of the Lord's Dealings with George Müller* (1837).

Bible Reading Notes

It has been said that you can make the Bible say anything you want it to, but that's only possible if you read the Bible out of context. We need to remember that each of the sixty-six books that make up the Bible had something to say to its original readers. Therefore, we have to make sure that what we understand is not something that the original writer did not intend. This is where a good set of Bible reading notes comes in handy, especially for new Christians.

When I first became a Christian, someone kindly gave me some Bible reading notes. They were invaluable. It was like having a pastor sitting by my side and taking me through the meaning of a passage. Their knowledge and research enabled me to understand the historical context of a passage. This greater understanding in turn enabled me to draw out the richness of the passage. Without doubt a good set of notes assists you to explore the Bible with greater confidence, particularly some of the harder books.

Over the years I have used many different Bible reading notes. My preference is those that work through a book of the Bible. This enables you to grasp the flow of a book as well as understanding the historical setting. Occasionally, though, I divert for a while to some topical Bible reading notes which focus on particular themes. For example, I may use a study guide that takes a more in-depth look at the different aspects of the fruit of the Spirit. Or one which focuses on the Lord's Prayer over several days. Here are a few suggestions for Bible reading notes:

- *Explore*, which covers three months at a time (published by The Good Book Company)

- *Every Day with Jesus* by Selwyn Hughes, (published by CWR)

- *Read Mark Learn* by John Blanchard, which takes you through Mark's Gospel (published by Evangelical Press)

Memorising Scripture
Memorising Scripture is of immense benefit. Psalm 119 has much to say about memorising God's Word. Here are just three of its instructions:

- 'How can a young person stay on the path of purity? By living according to your word' (v. 9)

- 'I have hidden your word in my heart that I might not sin against you' (v. 11)

- 'Your word is a lamp for my feet, a light on my path' (v. 105)

Clearly memorising Scripture is beneficial to the believer, yet how many verses of Scripture (other than John 3:16) do you know off by heart? For many people the answer will probably be very few. So here are some tips on how to memorise Scripture. First, select a verse, for example Proverbs 3:5–6, Isaiah 43:1–3, Psalm 73:25, Romans 8:28 or Colossians 1:21–22. Next, write it on a card and place it somewhere visible. You could place it by the bathroom mirror where you can look at it while cleaning your teeth. Alternatively, photograph it on your mobile phone and meditate on it while travelling to work, or waiting for the kettle to boil. You will be amazed how many pockets of redundant time you could redeem for memorising Scripture. Even if you spent a week learning just one verse, in a year you could potentially learn fifty-two verses! That's an incredible bank of wisdom and encouragement from which to draw. Even memorising one verse a month would prove to be enriching to your soul – give it a go!

Jesus said to his disciples that the Holy Spirit will 'teach you all things and will *remind* you of everything I have said to you' (John 14:26, my italics). But please note that the Holy Spirit can only remind us of things that we have taken the time and trouble to read and learn for ourselves! So if we want the Spirit to remind us of Scripture, then we need to invest time in depositing Scripture into our memory banks so that he has something to draw upon. As one pastor used to say, 'If you were empty headed before you were filled with the Spirit, you will be empty headed afterwards!'

Meditation on Scripture

We memorise a verse or passage in order to learn *what it says*, but we meditate upon it in order to chew over *what it means*. Meditation, unlike memorising, involves grasping the depth and richness of Bible verses. Small portions of Scripture are best for this.

Meditation is something which God encouraged his people to do. Consider these passages of Scripture:

> *Keep this Book of the Law always on your lips; meditate on it day and night, so that you may be careful to do everything written in it. Then you will be prosperous and successful (Josh. 1:8).*

> *Blessed is the one who does not walk in step with the wicked or stand in the way that sinners take or sit in the company of mockers, but whose delight is in the law of the L*ORD*, and who meditates on his law day and night. That person is like a tree planted by streams of water, which yields its fruit in season and whose leaf does not wither – whatever they do prospers (Ps. 1:1–3).*

Basil Pennington described the process of Bible meditation in this way:

It is not a question of reading a paragraph, a page or a chapter. It is, rather, sitting down with a friend, the Lord, and letting Him speak to us. We listen. And if what He says in the first word or the first sentence strikes us, we stop and let it sink in. We relish it. We respond from our heart. We enjoy it to the full before we move on. There is no hurry. We are sitting with our friend ... We let Him speak. We really listen.[4]

Bible meditation is an unhurried saturation in the Word of God. It is a deep pondering on every word found in a verse, allowing each one to feed and influence our soul.

Marked Scriptures

Call me old fashioned if you like, but I personally believe that every Christian ought to own a physical copy of the Bible rather than just an electronic version on their phone. The Bible I use for my devotions is rather dog-eared now as I bought it when I first became a Christian. If you were to look at it, you would find there is

---

[4.] Stephen Eyre, *Time with God* (IVP, 1995), p. 99.

hardly a page which doesn't contain verses that are highlighted, underlined, or with a little note by the side in the margin. In a way my Bible is a living journal, a record of verses which stood out for my encouragement. As a result, I know my way around it. For example, I know that Isaiah 55 is located on the left-hand page!

If I ever feel despondent for any reason, I find my eyes drawn to some of those underlined passages and receive great comfort from them. I believe that God would rather I had a marked and read Bible than an unmarked and unread one. Why not try underlining some of the verses that stand out for you!

3. PRAYER

We have already seen that Bible reading and prayer go hand in hand. God speaks to us when we read the Scriptures and we respond to him through prayer. It shouldn't surprise us that the one fuels the other.

How Should I Speak?

Samuel Chadwick said, 'Prayer is not a collection of balanced phrases; it is the pouring out of the soul.' God looks at heartfelt prayers. He doesn't mind if they are short and simple. The important thing is that they come from pure motives and are sincere. Indeed, Jesus gave the following guidance to his disciples: 'And when you pray, do not keep on babbling like pagans, for they think they will be heard because of their many words' (Mt. 6:7). It is the sincerity rather than the length of our prayers that gets God's attention.

As I have mentioned before, most of my praying is not verbalised audibly but rather flows silently from my heart. Sometimes I have even prayed to the Lord with sighs and tears because words were insufficient to express the burden in my heart. As someone once said, 'Tears are liquid prayers.'

What Do I Pray About?

Pray about anything and everything: not just yourself but also your family, friends, work and church, as well as the world. Pray for those who are not yet believers and for missionaries reaching those in other countries. If you pray just about yourself, you will become introspective and selfish. Remember that praying for others enables us to carry another person's burden before the Lord and be more Christ-like. The Apostle Paul is a perfect example of this: he often prayed for others even though he himself was in prison and in need of prayer (Eph. 1:15–23; 3:14–21; 2 Tim. 1:3–7).

The Benefits of a Prayer List

I would encourage every Christian to have a prayer list of one sort or another. This is a way of recording people you would like to pray for and any specific prayer requests. Many people, myself included, use the excellent PrayerMate app to help organise our prayer lists. PrayerMate also provides plenty of resources to fuel your prayers.

Here are three good reasons for keeping a prayer list:

1. We Have Poor Memories

Having a prayer list helps us to remember certain people, needs or organisations which we might otherwise neglect through forgetfulness.

2. It Assists Us with Our Concentration

Our list enables us to focus rather than drift in our praying. We can see who and what to pray for, rather than wasting time thinking, 'Oh, what am I going to pray about today?'

3. It Keeps Us Thankful

As we see the Lord answer our prayers, we are more likely to remember to thank him (Phil. 4:6). That also encourages us to pray all the more as we observe God at work.

A Prayer Structure

Many Christians find this acronym ACTS useful for guiding their prayers:

- Adoration
- Confession
- Thanksgiving
- Supplication

Adoration

Start by worshipping and adoring the Lord, thanking him for who he is. For when we affirm God's attributes, we ourselves grasp that there is no problem too great or small for him to handle. Affirming God's greatness increases our faith to trust him with our needs. Perhaps you may like to read a psalm or hymn to assist you in reflecting upon his majesty and might.

Confession

John Calvin used to pray at the end of his sermons, 'Lord, help us to hate our sins enough to turn from them.' Within your time of prayer you should bring to God those things that you know you need to ask for his forgiveness. You might want to use Psalms 32 or 51 to help you do this. Remember always to claim from God the cleansing power of the blood of Jesus and then leave your sin at the cross (1 John 1:9). Don't spend all of your time wallowing in self-pity. Christ longs to forgive you and for you to live in the light of that forgiveness (1 John 2:1–2).

Thanksgiving

Thank God for answers to prayer and for his goodness and daily provision. This is where keeping a prayer list or a journal proves useful because there are so many answers to prayer for which we often forget to thank the Lord (Phil. 4:6).

Supplication

Bring to God your concerns for the day, including your family, friends, work colleagues or members of your church fellowship who have particular needs.

As well as praying for those in our family and fellowship, I believe that every Christian ought to pray for those on the mission field too. Missionaries have made great sacrifices to serve the Lord overseas. They are far from the support structures and church fellowship which we ourselves enjoy. Some may even be serving in very dangerous countries where their lives are at risk. World mission is a crucial part of God's work which we need to support in prayer (see Mt. 28:19–20).

As part of your prayers, remember to pray also about your own opportunities for witnessing where you live and work. I always encourage Christians to be praying for at least five unconverted people whom they know, asking that they would come to saving faith in

Christ. Nothing encourages you to pray more than when someone whom you have been praying for surrenders their life to Jesus.

Once I have prayed through my list, I sometimes take a moment just to 'wait upon the Lord' to see if he will prompt me to pray about someone in particular. If this happens, I may send that person a text or email to ask if they are all right. Sometimes I feel led to tell them I had a burden to pray for them. More often than not, the person in question will tell me just how timely and encouraging that prayer was.

Remember Prayer Is Work

Prayer can be hard work. Paul said that Epaphras was 'always wrestling in prayer' for the Colossian believers (Col. 4:12). Without doubt there will be times when praying about something feels like a wrestling match. I have found this to be particularly true when praying for the unconverted, for the Devil will do everything he can to discourage us from evangelism. But persevere because, as the hymn-writer William Cowper said, 'Satan trembles when he sees the weakest saint upon his knees.' Prayer is one of the most powerful weapons in the armoury of the Christian and we must use it!

5

COMMON PROBLEMS WHICH AFFECT OUR QUIET TIME

Most people at some point in their Christian life will have difficulty in either establishing or maintaining a regular Quiet Time. There can be many reasons for this: some are spiritual, others are due to unavoidable circumstances of life.

FEELING UNWORTHY

The Devil doesn't want you to spend time with God and the two questions that he often sows into our mind are these: 'Is it really worth it?' and 'Will God listen to such an unholy person as you?' The answer is 'Yes' to both. The very fact that the Devil asks, 'Is it really worth it?'

is proof that it *is* worthwhile. He wants to rob you of vital contact with God, which every Christian needs to remain strong. In answer to the second question, always remember that even at our holiest moments we are only ever worthy to enter God's presence because of what Jesus achieved on the cross. So enjoy a Quiet Time because God loved you before you ever loved him (Rom. 5:8), let alone began your devotional times.

NOT BEING ABLE TO ENJOY A LENGTHY QUIET TIME

Parents with young children often feel guilty because they're unable to spend quality time with God. God understands! You are juggling your life around demanding and needy children, who throw tantrums just when you need it least. So parents should never feel guilty about taking only five minutes here or there staggered throughout their challenging day. Just take time when and where you can. Accept that, for a few years at least, your normal routine might be not having any routine at all. Remember too, though, that this is a season of life, not a sentence, and seasons do change – eventually!

MISSING A QUIET TIME

As Christians we know that we are saved by faith in Christ alone and not by our good works. However, we can still slip into a works mentality when it comes to our Quiet Times. For example, we might miss time with God one day and promise to spend twice as long with him the next as compensation! I would advise against this approach because you can't win God's favour that way. The cross is the only bargaining power we have with God, and he has already accepted that! Simply enjoy your usual Quiet Time the next day (see Lam. 3:19–23).

A DRY QUIET TIME

Have you ever picked up your Bible and, after reading it, felt you didn't receive much? If so, you are not alone. It's fair to say that some passages of Scripture are easier to understand and glean something from than others. For instance, reading through the Levitical laws can feel like wading through legalistic treacle! When faced with a more demanding book of the Bible like that, I would suggest using Bible reading notes where someone provides helpful insights along the way.

If your Bible reading is becoming a strain on the brain rather than fuel for the soul, then try a different book of the Bible for a while, such as a Gospel or the Psalms. You can always return to the more demanding books at a later date. You will find that alternating between New and Old Testament books will probably be beneficial to grasping the whole counsel of God's Word.

BITTERNESS AGAINST ANOTHER BELIEVER

Holding a grudge against a fellow Christian is a sure way of impeding us from receiving from God. Perhaps that's why Jesus said, 'And when you stand praying, if you hold anything against anyone, forgive them, so that your Father in heaven may forgive you your sins' (Mark 11:25). Bitterness can be a barrier to our worship, our witness and our prayers. We must learn to keep short accounts with people so that the ungrieved Holy Spirit can work within us.

The Apostle Paul was at pains to emphasise this very point to the church at Ephesus when he wrote, 'And do not grieve the Holy Spirit of God, with whom you were sealed for the day of redemption. Get rid of all bitterness, rage and anger, brawling and slander, along with every form of malice. Be kind and compassionate to one another, forgiving each other, just as in Christ God forgave you' (Eph. 4:30–32). The Holy Spirit is essential to the believer: he helps us to pray (Rom. 8:26; Jude 20) and to live the Christian life (John 14:26; 16:13; 2 Tim. 1:14). But the Holy Spirit is also sensitive, and if we harbour bitterness, then he will be grieved within us. We therefore need to forgive others, just as in Christ God forgives us.

UNCONFESSED SIN

There can be nothing more damaging to our walk with God than unrepented sin. 'Sin is essentially a departure from God,' as Martin Luther wrote. Sin causes us to feel alienated from God. This is echoed by the prophet Isaiah who wrote, 'But your iniquities have separated you from your God; your sins have hidden his face from you, so that he will not hear' (Is. 59:2). Sin caused Adam and Eve to hide from the Lord in the Garden of Eden (Gen. 3:10), and it will cause us to hide from the Lord too.

One way we hide is by not reading the Bible, for fear that God will expose us further. But I would urge you to come out from your bush, confess your failings and seek God's forgiveness. He is far more willing to offer you forgiveness than you might dare think. God would rather you draw near to him in a mess and looking for mercy, than not draw near to him at all (Jas. 4:8).

SO JUST DO IT!

'Just do it!' was the slogan used by Nike, the famous sports brand, but it ought to be written on every believer's Bible. There will be times when you won't feel like having a Quiet Time but remember that these devotional times enable God to speak to you. Not having one almost guarantees his silence!

6

SOME TIPS
TO TRY OUT

I want this book to be as practical to the reader as possible, so here are some suggestions to help you with your devotional life.

READ THE BIBLE

That may sound rather obvious, but I stress it because we can end up reading devotional books, study notes and commentaries more than we do the actual Bible itself. Reading devotional books must never take the place of reading the Bible.

GET UP EARLIER TO HAVE A
QUIET TIME

I'm sure getting up early is something that we have all vowed to do at some point, but somehow the intention never became a reality! So I suggest that you begin by setting your alarm just five minutes earlier in the morning. After a week, move it a further five minutes earlier. Within four weeks you will be rising twenty minutes earlier in the morning and your body clock will have had time to adjust.

If you would like to have your Quiet Time in the morning but are conscious of being late for work because of traffic, then try leaving early so that you arrive at work half an hour before everyone else. That way you can have a Quiet Time in the office before everyone else arrives. It may also be a means of witnessing to your work mates, if they ever ask you why you're in early. You might also miss some of the traffic too!

DEAL WITH INVADING THOUGHTS

Try writing down everything that is running through your mind, such as meetings you need to attend or people with whom you need to speak. This will gradually free you from worrying about forgetting those particular things. Then talk to your heavenly Father about your to-do list.

REFLECT ON A FAVOURITE HYMN OR LISTEN TO A WORSHIP SONG

Why not begin your devotional time by reading the words of a hymn, or worship song, to help you focus on the majesty of God. I find hymns especially helpful as they are full of inspiring truths. Many hymns are like mini sermons, carrying theology in song.

Being a musician, I occasionally start my devotions by singing worship songs, but you could also listen to one on Spotify or YouTube. Scripture instructs us to be 'speaking to one another with psalms, hymns, and songs from the Spirit' (Eph. 5:19).

EMBRACE VARIETY

Try using different Bible reading notes. For example, I sometimes use Selwyn Hughes' *Every Day with Jesus*, which tends to be topical, meaning it can jump around different parts of the Bible. Then for a while I use some of the *Explore* Bible reading notes, which take you through a book of the Bible. Alternatively, as you approach the seasons of Advent or Lent, you might like to use one of Tim Chester's excellent devotional books.

ASK QUESTIONS

Questions are like keys: they can unlock doors that lead to interesting places. It's helpful to have some key questions at the back of your mind when considering any passage of Scripture. They help you dig out nuggets of gold from the mine of God's Word. Examples are:

- What is happening in this passage?

- Why is it happening?

- Is there a truth I need to apply?

- Is there a promise that I can keep?

- Is there an action I need to take?

- Is there a habit I need to stop?

- Is there an encouragement I can take?

- Is there a sin I need to confess?

- Is there something about God that I need to learn?

- Is there a challenge to my life I need to take on board?

You may want to keep a journal of the things that God teaches you from his Word.

USE PRAYERS IN THE BIBLE TO FUEL YOUR OWN PRAYERS

I have met people who say, 'Once I have prayed for myself and my family, I can't think of anything else to pray about!' If that describes you, then take heart: there is so much to pray about! Prayers from the Bible are a wonderful starting point. For example, Colossians 1:9–14 or Ephesians 3:14–19 give ideas of things to pray into your own life as well as the life of another believer.

The PrayerMate app also provides a host of resources to fuel your prayers. Try praying for people in your house group, your congregation, your church staff or missionaries. You might even pray for a few items from the BBC news. That should be enough to keep you going!

HELP, I HAVE TOO MUCH TO PRAY ABOUT!

I receive two or three prayer letters from various organisations each week in my email. The problem is that every one of them has valid prayer requests, which I used to feel guilty ignoring. But a missionary friend of mine helpfully told me that his practice is to read a prayer letter, spend five minutes praying for the requests, then delete it! A missionary would rather you pray earnestly for them for five minutes than not pray at all.

THE BIBLE AS FOOD FOR THOUGHT

Why not use your lunch break to chew over the Word of God as well as your sandwiches! Or eat your breakfast with your Bible open on the table at the same time. That would give a whole new meaning to the verse 'Man shall not live on bread alone, but on every word that comes from the mouth of God' (Mt. 4:4).

MAKE USE OF EVERY OPPORTUNITY DURING THE DAY

Mobile phones with their various apps (like PrayerMate) make it extremely easy nowadays for you to take your prayer list to work with you. Why not pray during your journey to or from work. You might even pray during those redundant moments of time, for example, while waiting for someone to answer the phone or for the kettle to boil! Use these as extra opportunities to pray. Nehemiah was someone who often sent up arrow prayers while he worked (Neh. 2:4).

ENJOY A QUIET TIME ON THE MOVE

If you spend a lot of time in the car, why not download apps that enable you to listen to a Bible devotional as you drive. Nicky Gumbel has a free app called Bible in One Year, which I used while dropping my sons off to school.

BE CREATIVE IF YOU HAVE YOUNG CHILDREN

I know of one married couple who take turns to look after their children while the other goes off to have a Quiet Time. Sometimes the mum covers for the dad in the morning, then the dad returns the favour in the evening. One mother I know has an alternative approach: she involves her children in her Quiet Times. She encourages them to pray briefly, then reads a passage of Scripture with them. Obviously their attention span is limited, but it is still Bible time. It also means they are learning a good habit at an early age!

FIND A PRAYER PARTNER

Find a prayer partner who will ask you once a fortnight how your Quiet Times are going and how they have encouraged or challenged you. This enables you both to grow. Even if one of you is struggling with Quiet Times, the other can share something that the Lord had taught them. As I mentioned before, Proverbs describes that in this way: 'As iron sharpens iron, so one person sharpens another' (Prov. 27:17).

HAVE A 'QUIET DAY'

If you have never tried this, I would recommend it. Every three or four months set aside a day (or half a day) as a Quiet Day with the Lord. Head out to the hills (or somewhere else quiet) by yourself. Bring a picnic lunch, your Bible and a note pad. Then begin to talk to the Lord, reviewing your life in relation to him. List areas where you feel you need to grow in your character, gifts and priorities for God. Also review your prayer list. For example, you might sense that there are people that you should stop praying for. Equally, there may be people or situations that you add to your prayer list.

REMEMBER BLESSINGS FROM THE PAST

Many people highlight or underline passages in their Bibles that have blessed and encouraged them at some point in the past. My own Bible has many such underlinings. It is to those very same verses that I tend to return when feeling spiritually depleted. More often than not, a past blessing becomes a lifeline for the present, helping to revive my downcast heart. It's definitely worth building up some reserves of Scripture to reflect upon during the dry seasons of life.

READ A NEW TESTAMENT LETTER

Why not set aside some time to read an entire letter from the New Testament – after all, that was the way they were intended to be read! My wife and I once did this when we turned up to a church too early. We read out loud Paul's letter to the Ephesians, from start to finish, taking a chapter each. It only took us about twenty minutes. You can often glean far more from a letter when you have read it right the way through in one sitting.

7

USING THE LORD'S PRAYER AND THE PSALMS

What we call the Lord's Prayer is designed to be a model for our own praying. It's a skeleton prayer which we can flesh out. Within it we see every element that our own prayer time ought to contain, such as praise, thanksgiving, confession and supplication.

PRAYING THROUGH THE LORD'S PRAYER

Here is how I might use the Lord's Prayer as a model. The words in italics simply show my thought processes as I slowly pray through and am prompted by each phrase.

'Our Father, who art in heaven'

Thank God for who he is: *Thank you, Lord, that we can indeed call you 'Father'. In you we find our true identity, our sense of value and belonging. You are our provider and our protector. You dwell in heaven, yet you care for us here on earth.*

'Hallowed be thy name'

Pray that your life would honour God: *You are the great eternal God, who is worthy of all honour and praise. Therefore may my life today bring you joy, and may everything I do and say be honouring to your name.*

'Thy kingdom come, thy will be done, on earth as it is in heaven'

Pray for God's rule to be part of your daily life and our nation's life: *Lord, may your kingdom values be evident in my own life as well as that of my family. I pray for wise and God-honouring decisions to be taken by the leaders of our country. I pray that your glorious kingdom will continue to extend throughout the world as you bring more people to a saving knowledge of your Son, Jesus. Help us to be ready for that day when you return and your kingdom will come with power and glory.*

Also pray for those parts of the world suffering injustice or war – perhaps one or two specific situations that are in the news – for those working as missionaries and for the persecuted church.

'Give us this day our daily bread'

Thank the Lord for his provision in your life. There are so many things that God has blessed us with and yet we so easily take for granted. Gratitude is the way we show our appreciation to God: *Lord, I thank you for the spiritual and material comforts that you have blessed me with. I thank you for the daily provision of everything that I need to live and thrive. Every good gift is from you and I thank you for them all.*

'And forgive us our sins'

All sin is ultimately an offence against God, in addition to those we have wronged. Take time to examine your behaviour, actions and attitudes to see if there is anything that grieves the Lord. Ask his forgiveness for your unkind attitudes or hurtful words you have said to or about others. Pray for the opportunity to make amends and restore any broken relationships: *Lord forgive me for ...*

'As we forgive those who have sinned against us'

Take time to reflect on anyone who may have consciously or unconsciously offended you. Ask the Lord to give you the grace to forgive them. That might be hard to do, but such forgiveness is Christ-like. Remember that holding a grudge cripples us and grieves the Holy Spirit (see Eph. 4:30–31): *Lord, I forgive ... for ... Help me not to hold a grudge against them.*

'And lead us not into temptation'

Ask the Lord to give you the strength to avoid people, websites or places that cause you to stray from his ways (2 Cor. 10:4–5). Pray that the Holy Spirit would highlight anything you watch, listen to or do which might fuel sinful behaviour. Ask the Lord to show you if there are any unhealthy relationships you are developing of which he would not approve. Also ask him to preserve you from pride, greed or lust, which can cripple our souls: *Lord, guard my heart from straying from you, and give me strength to avoid acting upon any unhelpful thoughts.*

'But deliver us from evil'

Pray that God would protect you from the work of the evil one. Remember that 'the one who is in you is greater than the one who is in the world' (1 John 4:4). Satan has power, but the Lord has unlimited power. Through the blood of Jesus, the Devil has been overcome (1 Cor. 15:55; Col. 2:15; Rev. 12:11): *Lord, preserve me from the evils of this world and grant me the discernment to know your will and your ways. May I trust you to deliver me from the enemy's schemes.*

'For thine is the kingdom, the power and the glory, for ever and ever, Amen'

The Lord's kingdom, power and glory will ultimately prevail. His kingdom will come and all other kingdoms will go! Take heart as you face your day, for we look forward to Christ's return, when he will make all things new. This is the God who we are privileged to call our

Father in heaven. He will walk with us through every step of our day and every situation we will face: *Lord, help me to keep living my life in the light of eternity. Whatever I face may I never lose sight of your sovereignty in all situations. Keep my heart focused on that glorious day when Christ will return and make all things new.*

PRAYING THROUGH THE PSALMS

During times of trouble, Christians have turned to the Psalms more than to any other book in the Bible. In the Psalms we find people baring their hearts to God with raw honesty. They express emotions which reflect many of our own questions, doubts and struggles in life. The psalmists say the kind of things that we ourselves long to say. Howard Baker comments that in the Psalms:

> *God Himself has supplied a toolbox for constructing a meaningful prayer life. All of the formulas, acrostics and gimmicks to make praying simple and easy are exposed as shallow in the face of the pulsating reality, life and depth of the Psalms as a guide to prayer. I learn*

to pray by praying, and the Psalms provide the
pattern for me. As I pray, the Psalms leave their
mark on my soul until finally I find my own
prayers conforming to the original pattern.[5]

The Psalms teach us three things about prayer.

1. Praying Honestly

We are taught to pray honestly about our true
feelings and emotions. There is no need for us
to disguise our emotions before the Lord. We
can approach him with all the conflicts, fears
and doubts in the world – he will not turn us
away. Charlotte Elliott discovered this when she
penned the hymn 'Just as I Am', which includes
these lines: 'Just as I am, though tossed about
with many a conflict, many a doubt, fightings
within and fears without, O Lamb of God,
I come.'

2. Praying Comprehensively

The Psalms contain a wide spectrum of material
to focus our prayers upon. For instance, we are
encouraged to pray about the state of the nations

---

[5] Howard Baker, *Christianity Magazine*, October 1997.

(Ps. 2); to confess and repent of our sinfulness (Ps. 51); to seek forgiveness and cleansing (Ps. 32); to exalt God's glory (Ps. 8; 19); to praise God (Ps. 24; 33; 47); to find security in him (Ps. 3; 20; 23; 34); to pray against injustice (Ps. 12; 43); to give thanks (Ps. 21); and to express our longings (Ps. 42) ... and that's just in the first fifty psalms!

3. Praying in a God-centred Way

Often our prayers can be rather introspective, focusing only upon *our* problems, *our* needs and *our* desires. Yet we need to remember that God is infinitely bigger than our problems and therefore ought to be the main focal point of our prayers. Many psalms begin with the writer's whole horizon being filled with the issue they face, to such an extent that they cannot see beyond their problems. But once they include God in the picture, he begins to eclipse their troubles. He floods the darkness of the soul with penetrating brightness. He alone brings hope, where there was despair. And so, by the end of the psalm, the problems that dwarfed the psalmist have themselves been dwarfed by God.

The writer comes to the liberating realisation that although his problems may never disappear, the God whom he worships is larger still and will never leave him.

8

QUIET TIME STUDIES

The following Bible studies incorporate some of the elements that we have considered about what makes up a Quiet Time. They also touch upon some of the things that hinder us as well as inspire us in our Quiet Time. I trust that God will speak into your heart through them and encourage you.

STUDY 1:

PRIORITIES AND DISTRACTIONS

PREPARE YOUR HEART

Before you begin, write down on a piece of paper anything that is distracting you at this moment and that might rob you from focusing on God. Now take a moment to listen to and reflect upon the words of the song 'O for a Closer Walk with God' by William Cowper.

READ GOD'S WORD

Luke 10:38–42

If this passage had ended at verse 40, what would your initial reaction have been? Would you have viewed Mary as lazy and Martha as godly because Martha was doing all the hard work? After all, the work she was doing was to serve the Lord! When we see the Lord's reaction to Martha's plea in verses 41–42, we see a different perspective altogether. Instead of agreeing with Martha, Jesus lovingly corrected her: '"Martha, Martha," the Lord answered, "you are worried and upset about many things, but few things are needed – or indeed only one. Mary has chosen what is better, and it will not be taken away from her."'

Jesus was effectively teaching Martha that it's possible to do many things *for* the Lord and not spend adequate time *with* the Lord. Martha was so absorbed in showering Jesus with hospitality that she was clearly overdoing it on the catering side. Perhaps she was trying to impress him by cooking way more fancy dishes than was required, which was adding to her distress. Jesus would have been satisfied with one simple meal – so she could have spent time with him too, just like her sister Mary. The Lord wasn't condemning Martha for working, but rather for overworking. This squeezed out precious moments with him. But God doesn't want us to be workaholics any more than he wants us to be alcoholics!

Have you been so overfilling your diary (even through doing things for the Lord) that you find yourself too tired, too busy or too late to spend time with the Lord? How is your diary looking now? Are there things you need to drop so you can be in the presence of Jesus? Re-examine your priorities this week and see where adjustments need to be made. We can all find plenty of things to keep us busy, but the question is are they the most important things?

PRAY

Confess to the Lord if you have been overworking and robbing your soul of refreshing time with God. Ask the Lord to help you prioritise your life better.

STUDY 2:

YOU ARE BLESSED

PREPARE YOUR HEART

One of the greatest songs which has been penned in modern times is 'In Christ Alone' by Stuart Townend and Keith Getty. The words are deep and rich in theology. So prepare your heart by listening to this song, with the words in front of you. Ask the Lord, by his Holy Spirt, to bless your reading of his Word and your understanding of it.

READ GOD'S WORD

Ephesians 1:1–14

When my two boys, James and Ben, were just five and three years old, I remember them excitedly waking up on Christmas Day to see what was in each of their Christmas sacks. I still recall their wide eyes and shrieks of joy as they dipped their hand into their sack to pull out gifts. 'Look, I got a game!'

shouted one, followed by, 'Wow, a teddy bear!' from the other. And so this joyful exchange continued, as each rummaged deeper and deeper into their sacks, until every last gift was drawn. Even the orange at the very bottom was met with joy – I wish they were that easily pleased now!

In this passage the Apostle Paul was, in effect, dipping his hand into the sack of all the spiritual blessings he had in Christ. He was pulling each one out with wide-eyed wonder! It's as if he was saying, 'Wow, I'm chosen by God.' 'Look at this, I'm adopted into his family and called a son.' 'Look, I'm redeemed and have forgiveness from all my sin ... how amazing!' Paul continues in this vein right the way through the opening verses. In fact, in the original Greek these opening verses were one long sentence. Paul, like a child at Christmas, was bursting with excitement to tell the believers of all the blessings they had. Some blessings relate to our past, some to our present and others to our future; there are just so many.

How did Paul acquire these blessings? There is a recurring phrase which provides the answer: 'in him/Christ'. If you have accepted Christ as your personal Lord and Saviour, then you are 'in Christ' and have these blessings. Read and savour each of them for they are all yours. They are God's declarations over your life. Each one speaks of your new identity. Enjoy unpacking every single one of them.

PRAY

Underline all the blessings that you can identify from this passage. Dwell on each one, thanking God for what each means to your life.

BURN-OUT!

PREPARE YOUR HEART

Begin your devotion by listening to the song 'He Will Hold Me Fast' by Ada Ruth Habershon and Matt Merker. Then reflect for a moment on this: where is your sense of value in God's sight found? Is it in what you *do* or in who you *are*?

READ GOD'S WORD

1 Kings 19:1–18

Elijah was a prophet of God. His faith in the Lord's power enabled him to win a tremendous victory against the priests of the false god Baal (1 Kgs. 18). This resulted in the Israelites repenting and returning to follow God. Yet despite this great victory, we find Elijah in a desperately low state, wishing that he were dead (1 Kgs. 19:3–4). He didn't know it at the time but he was suffering from spiritual burn-out!

Have you ever felt like Elijah? Perhaps you are feeling like that right now. If so, what has led you to that point? Look at the way God deals with Elijah in verses 5–9. Do you notice anything surprising? God doesn't lecture him on his faithlessness, nor tell him to pull himself together. Instead God encourages Elijah to ... rest! That tells me that God is far more interested in the worker than the work. Elijah was of more value to God than his ministry. Pause for a moment and read my last sentence again because some of you need to hear this important truth. Never forget that you are more valuable to God than the work or ministry that you are doing. Jesus died on the cross for you; he didn't die on the cross for the work you do. Too many people think that their value is based on what they do, rather than on who they are.

The Lord doesn't leave Elijah as a burned-out shell of a man, but tenderly restores him by feeding him and encouraging him to sleep.

Clearly God knew that Elijah's first need was physical. Only once Elijah had adequately rested did God move on to his spiritual needs. How moving it is that God speaks to Elijah in 'a gentle whisper' (v. 12). This is the language of tenderness and proximity: you only need to whisper when you are close to someone. God was seeking to comfort Elijah, like a mother saying, 'Hush now, it's alright' to her distressed child.

Elijah felt crushed in spirit and had written himself off – but this passage shows us that God doesn't have scrap heaps, only restoration yards!

PRAY

Unlike the world's love, God's love for you is not based on how successful you are, but on whose you are. Thank him for that! However much you feel like you are flagging or you are a failure, God remains loyal in his love towards you. He wants to restore you. Why not use the words of the hymn 'Just as I Am' by Charlotte Elliott to aid your prayers.

STUDY 4:

BACK TO BASICS

PREPARE YOUR HEART

Meditate for a moment on these words of Jesus: 'Whoever wants to be my disciple must deny themselves and take up their cross daily and follow me' (Luke 9:23). Now reflect upon how that verse impacts your life when you substitute your own name in place of the word 'whoever'.

READ GOD'S WORD

Luke 9:18–27

In the Roman-occupied Israel of Christ's time the cross meant only one thing – death. People understood that anyone carrying a cross out of the city was not coming back. In this passage Jesus used the phrase to 'take up' your 'cross' to refer to the cost of commitment for those who wished to follow him. It meant denying their rights to their own lives, surrendering them willingly, totally and freely to him. That, after all, is exactly what Christ did for us – he surrendered his life to spare us from the punishment our sins rightfully deserved. As C.T. Studd, the great missionary, said, 'If Jesus Christ be God and gave himself for me, then no sacrifice can be too great for me to make for him.'

Whoever you are, and however long you have been a Christian, humbly and honestly examine your life. Ask yourself if Jesus is still Lord over your life, or whether you have relegated him to the edges of your life. Is he still the one to whom you bow the knee every morning, submitting to his will, or do you expect him to submit to your will? Christ has never drifted in his commitment towards you, but perhaps you have drifted from your commitment towards him. If that's the case, come to him in fresh surrender because Jesus wants followers, not admirers. He needs to be in the driving seat of your life – not the passenger seat –

otherwise you'll miss out on the journey that he planned for you (Ps. 23).

You might also like to look up Matthew 4:18–22 and Romans 12:1–2.

PRAY

Perhaps use the Apostle Paul's words in Philippians 3:7–14 as a basis for prayer for your own life. One missionary used to pray this: 'Every day that I wake up, my first prayer is to die to my own selfish desires and to surrender my life afresh to Christ as my Lord and Saviour.' May this be true of your life too.

LIGHT IN TIMES OF DARKNESS

PREPARE YOUR HEART

Begin by reading and reflecting on Psalm 23. Thank the Lord that he is your Shepherd and as such will protect and provide for you now, as he has done in the past. Perhaps also read the words of the hymn 'All the Way My Saviour Leads Me' by Fanny J. Crosby.

READ GOD'S WORD

Psalm 27

This psalm was written by David shortly after a time of persecution – perhaps when Saul was pursuing David, or when his own son Absalom rebelled against him (2 Sam. 15). One thing is certain: David knew that his ultimate security lay not in his own, limited strength, but in the Lord's unlimited strength. The circumstances looked very bleak for

David – 'the wicked advance against me to devour me' (v. 2), 'an army besiege me' (v. 3) – but when he earnestly turned to the Lord, he found hope in those dark times.

Have you ever felt that God has forgotten you or abandoned you? Look again at verses 7–12. David began by pleading with the Lord not to ignore him in his moment of need. Then David found this incredible reassurance: 'Though my father and mother forsake me, the LORD will receive me' (v. 10). David realised the astonishing truth that God would never forsake him, even if his own family members did. God alone is the perfect parent; he remains utterly loyal and loving towards his children, irrespective of the challenges they are facing. With this reassurance David penned the last two verses, expressing his total confidence in God. He firmly believed that whatever adversity he faced, he would be facing it with God.

Throughout history the Lord has carried his people through many dangers and difficulties. His arms have been steady, his presence has been close and his faithfulness has never wavered for one moment. That means he will be there for you too. Why not write down the verse from this psalm that encourages you the most, then reflect on it throughout today.

PRAY

As you pray for any difficult circumstances that you are currently facing, ask God to overwhelm you with his peace. If God doesn't change your circumstances, he may be trying to change you to face your circumstances. Try to discern what Christ-like attitudes or fruit of the Spirit he might be wanting to develop in you through this challenging time. Reflect on Galatians 5:22–23 and Romans 5:1–5.

GOD OUR PROVIDER

PREPARE YOUR HEART

If possible, go outside and sit in the garden. Before you open your Bible, look around you at God's creation. Consider the variety of plants, trees, birds and insects. Observe the colours and textures in all their diversity. Look up above at the clouds sailing on the ocean of sky. Everything you see, no matter how large or small, is at this very moment totally dependent upon God's sustaining power to keep it alive and in its place (Heb. 1:3). That is utterly amazing, isn't it? Spend some time praising God for his majesty and power.

READ GOD'S WORD

Psalm 19:1–6

David sat for a moment, just as you have done, and marvelled at God's creation. He recognised that creation itself declares there is a God who made this universe, planning it to the finest detail. Incredible though it may seem, God made this world for us to enjoy because he considers us the most important part of his creation. We have the capacity to relate to God in a way that no other creature can. We alone can appreciate and worship him. We alone have been made in his image (Gen. 1:26).

Psalm 19:7–11
The Lord has provided us with a beautiful planet to enjoy and look after. Through cultivating the land, we produce food for our bodies. But God didn't create us simply to survive in this world; he wants us to thrive! So God has provided his written Word, which feeds and nourishes our souls, and provides guidance so that we can live in a way that honours him. Read these verses again, noting how many benefits are obtained from reading his Word. Underline them. Pause and meditate for a moment on each phrase as you chew over the value of God's Word to

our soul's well-being. The Word of God is to our souls what food, water and air are to our bodies: we can't thrive without it!

Psalm 19:12–14

Notice how David turns from adoration (vv. 1–6) to instruction (vv. 7–11). This then leads him to confession (vv. 12–14). So often reading God's Word is like switching a spotlight on our soul. The Lord highlights things in our lives which hinder us from fellowship with him. He encourages us to confess our sin – both our deliberate wrongs (v. 12) and those hidden faults of which we may be unaware (v. 14). The blood of Jesus has the power to cleanse us from every sin to the extent that God can look upon us as being blameless and innocent (v. 13). Come to the Lord now, confessing any sin and accepting his cleansing.

PRAY

Thank God for all his provision in your life. Marvel at this amazing world in which we live, with its staggering beauty and incredible diversity of life. Praise God for his Word that gives such rich food for your soul.

STUDY 7:

THE FREEDOM
OF FORGIVENESS

PREPARE YOUR HEART

Many people only say the Lord's Prayer at church on Sundays, and even then it is often mechanically recited rather than earnestly prayed. Why not take time now to slowly and considerately pray through it. Then move on to ponder these words: 'Blessed is the one whose transgressions are forgiven, whose sins are covered. Blessed is the one whose sin the LORD does not count against them and in whose spirit is no deceit' (Ps. 32:1–2). Next re-read these verses, putting your own name in place of the words 'one' or 'them'. Isn't that reassuring? If you have truly asked the Lord to forgive you for your sin, then you have God's word that all is forgiven!

READ GOD'S WORD

Colossians 1:15–23

When I first became a Christian, my pastor invited a group of new converts to his home. It was a cold November night and we huddled round an open fire. He passed round a piece of paper and pen, and asked us to write down what we most regretted doing in our lives. Once we had finished, he asked us to fold up the paper and place it in the paper cup in his hand. Nervously we did so, worrying what he might do with them. He tossed the scraps of paper around the cup with his finger. Then, after a long silence, he said, 'This is exactly what happened to your sin when you put your trust in Jesus' sacrificial death on the cross', and the threw the paper cup into the fire! Needless to say we all breathed a sigh of relief. Our individual guilt and shame had gone – forever! It felt so good! A vast weight had been lifted.

The truth of God's forgiveness hit home to me in a fresh way that night. My sin was no longer remembered in the mind of

God. He chose to remember it no more. So completely did he forgive me that he views me as 'holy in his sight, without blemish and free from accusation' (v. 22). How incredible! That night I sang my heart out to the Lord, thanking him for his mercy and love towards me.

PRAY

The Lord's Prayer encourages us to seek forgiveness as well as to offer it to those who have sinned against us. That's not always easy to do, but forgiveness is the most liberating thing in the world. As long as you hold a grudge against someone, you yourself will remain somewhat spiritually impoverished. Your bitterness towards them will do you no good. Perhaps there are people who you need to forgive. If so, release your offenders and your own heart from bitterness.

STUDY 8:

AMAZED BY GRACE

PREPARE YOUR HEART

It's incredible to think that 'Amazing Grace' is the most recorded song of all time. Listen to one recording of it, reading the lyrics as you do. Reflect on each line, thanking God for the truths they contain.

READ GOD'S WORD

Ephesians 2:1-10

The words to 'Amazing Grace' were written in 1772 by a former slave trader, John Newton, who, following his conversion to Christ, became a gospel minister. So transformed was his life that he made it his aim both to win people to Jesus Christ and to work for the abolition of slavery. What a transformation!

The Apostle Paul tells us that an amazing transformation has happened to us. We were once dead in our sins and lifeless towards God. We followed our own selfish desires and were influenced by the evil one (vv. 1–3). We were in a miserable rebellious state and came under God's righteous judgement. As John Newton expressed it, we were wretched, blind and lost.

But that was before God's amazing grace came crashing into our lives. It woke us up to our desperate plight and enabled us to cry out to God. What we found was generous mercy, freely given to us through Christ. On the cross Jesus took the punishment for our rebellion and sin upon himself. He did this as a gracious act of generous love in order to offer us his mercy. Grace is often described as undeserved favour, while mercy is described as undeserved forgiveness. God's grace and mercy cannot be earned by our good works; they can only be received through our acceptance of Christ.

Our place in heaven is not based on our own merits. We contribute nothing to our salvation. Our place in heaven has been secured entirely through the finished work of Christ's death and resurrection. It's by our trust in him alone that we have certainty of entering heaven. As a result, the Apostle Paul could confidently say, 'God raised us up and seated us with him in the heavenly realms' (v. 6). That verse always makes me think about the seating plan at a wedding. Perhaps, like me, you have attended a wedding but then been unsure if you accepted the wedding dinner invite. You desperately scan the seating plan to see if you spot your name, and when you do, you're so relieved! God wants us to be assured that if we have accepted Christ as our Saviour and Lord, then we are on his seating plan!

PRAY

Thank God for his amazing grace that drew you from darkness into his glorious light. Thank him that he breathed spiritual life into your dead soul. Praise him that your place in heaven is guaranteed because of Christ and not because of your good works.

Although we are not saved *by* our works, we are saved to *do* good works, which God has prepared in advance for us to do (v. 10). Why not pray about areas in your church where God might be calling you to serve. Ask your church leaders where you might best use your gifts and abilities.

Publishing

a division of 10 of those.com

10Publishing is the publishing house of **10ofThose**. It is committed to producing quality Christian resources that are biblical and accessible.

www.10ofthose.com is our online retail arm selling thousands of quality books at discounted prices.

For information contact: **info@10ofthose.com** or check out our website: **www.10ofthose.com**